Gilbert's
Best Jokes on Earth

Gilbert's
Best Jokes on Earth

GRAHAM MARKS &
CHRISTOPHER MAYNARD

ILLUSTRATED BY DAVID SIMONDS

GILBERT'S BEST JOKES ON EARTH

A CORGI BOOK 0 552 52535 9

Originally published in Great Britain by
Corgi Books

PRINTING HISTORY
Corgi edition published 1988
Corgi edition reprinted 1988

Typeset by Maggie Spooner Typesetting, London

Corgi Books are published by Transworld Publishers Ltd., 61–63 Uxbridge Road, Ealing, London W5 5SA, in Australia by Transworld Publishers (Aust.) Pty. Ltd., 15–23 Helles Avenue, Moorebank, NSW 2170, and in New Zealand by Transworld Publishers (N.Z.) Ltd., Cnr. Mosell and Waipareira Avenues, Henderson, Auckland.

Printed and bound in Great Britain by
Cox & Wyman Ltd., Reading, Berks.

CONTENTS

INGREDIENTS: WATER (inc. TEARS, E397), WOOD PULP, VEGETABLE MATTER IN VARIABLE PROPORTIONS, INK, BLACK, WHITE, DRAWINGS, RUTABAGA, JOKES, BLOOD, OIL (Midnight, E412), MONOSODIUM GLUTAMATE.

Best Before: See Date on Lid.

8oz 227g ℮

1. Cannibal Jokes

The Birthday Present

Did you hear the one about the man who went into a shop and told the assistant he wanted to buy his sister a terrific egg-timer for her birthday?

'Oh, that *will* be a nice surprise!' said the shop assistant.

'Not really,' he replied. 'She's expecting a two-week holiday in the Bahamas!'

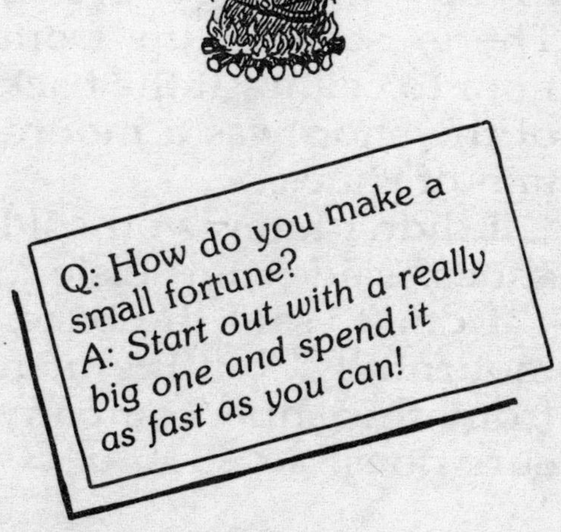

Lace-up Loaves

Aunt Elsie went to her local baker's the other day to buy a loaf of bread. There, stacked up from floor to ceiling at the back of the shop was a mountain of shoes.

'I didn't know you sold shoes,' said Aunt Elsie.

'I don't,' said the baker mournfully, 'but the man from the shoe company sure does!'

Here's a message for all those people who love cricket.
There isn't any!

Doctoring the Evidence

Young Bert went to the doctor's one day, feeling a little fire-engine red about the nose.

'I'm not at all well,' he told the white-coated quack.

'I think there's nothing wrong with you that a bit of hard work wouldn't cure!' was the doctor's reply.

'I demand a second opinion!' insisted Bert.

'OK. You're as ugly as a mouldy old Stilton too!' said the doctor.

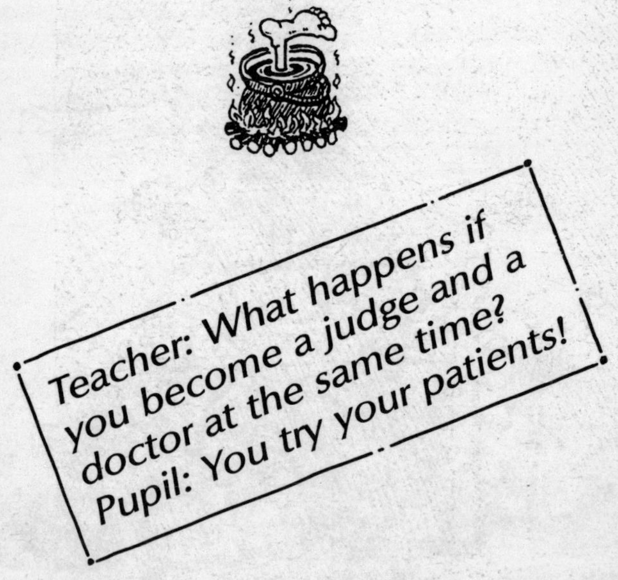

I SAY, I SAY, I SAY . . .

I love exercise, especially cross-country runs in the rain when they're being run by someone I don't like.

Teacher: If the people who live in Poland are called Poles, what do you call people who live in Holland?
Pupil: Dutch!

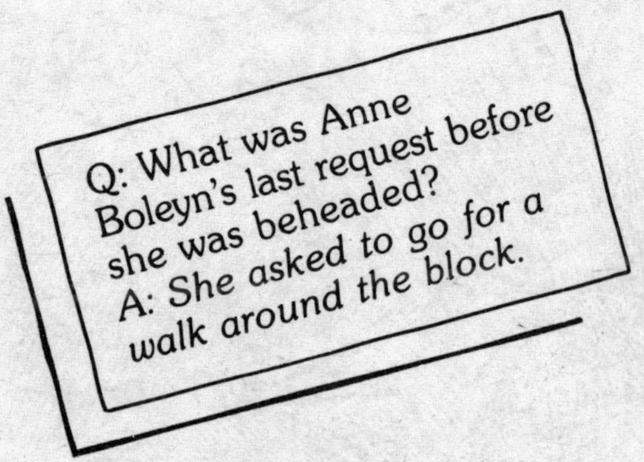

Heavy Problem

A woman took a parcel to the post office the other day. The fellow behind the counter told her it was too heavy and to put more stamps on it.

'Is that supposed to make it lighter?' she asked.

'Ere!
What's the largest
tree in the world
called?
Derek.

A Slice of Life

The other day, Derek went into Costas' café and ordered a cheese and onion sandwich. When the waitress brought it, he asked her to change it for a doughnut, which he ate. As he was about to leave, Costas yelled at him to pay for the doughnut.

'What do you mean?' Derek said. 'I gave you a cheese and onion sandwich for the doughnut!'

'But you didn't pay for the sandwich!' said Costas.

'But I didn't eat it,' Derek replied, 'so why should I pay for it?'

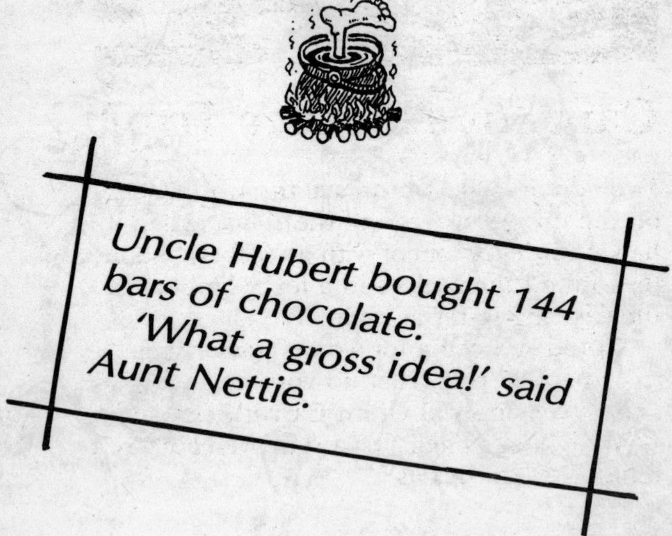

2. Fat Frank Jokes

Care for Another Trip?

Two young chaps out to see the world were on the maiden voyage of the *Titanic* when it had its little argument with an iceberg. Soon they found themselves in a leaky lifeboat in the freezing water at night.

'Could've been a lot worse,' says Nigel.

'Worse! Worse! What do you mean, *worse?*' yells his old chum Carruthers.

'Well,' says Nigel, 'for a start we could've bought return tickets!'

Big Kid: If babies were allowed to join the army, where would they go?
Little Kid: Into the infantry!
Big Kid: And if they were promoted and then did a big one in their nappies, what would you call it?
Little Kid: A sergeants' mess!

Mean Old Sod

There was an old miser in Ashby-de-la-Zouch who bought his wife a plot at the cemetery for her birthday last year. This year he didn't buy her a thing.

When she asked him why, he said it was because she hadn't used last year's present!

Q: What do you get when you cross a kangaroo with a sheep?
A: Lamb chops that leap right off the plate.

Good News

A man ran over to his neighbour's house and knocked on the door.

'I've got some good news, and I've got some bad news. You've just won a million pounds!'

'Blimey!' said the neighbour. 'What's the bad news?'

'I'm lying!' replied the man.

Teacher: What can trot along a road on its head?
Pupil: A nail in a horseshoe.

I SAY, I SAY, I SAY . . .

Laugh and the world laughs with you — weep and you wet your face!

True Confessions

Two partners had been in business together for years, when suddenly one of them became seriously ill. As the fellow slowly grew weaker, his partner came to the hospital to visit him.

'You look terrible,' he said in his most sympathetic voice.

'I feel terrible too,' said the dying man. 'Look. Before I go, I've a confession to make. I've been stealing money from the company for years.'

'Don't worry anymore, it's all right,' murmured his partner.

'You're a saint to be so forgiving,' said the dying man.

'Not really,' smiled the partner, 'it was me who poisoned you!'

I say, I say, I say. My dog hasn't got a nose!
So it was him I saw in the building society!

Teacher: When Queen Beatrix of the Netherlands gets sick, what does she suffer from?
Pupil: Dutch Realm Disease.

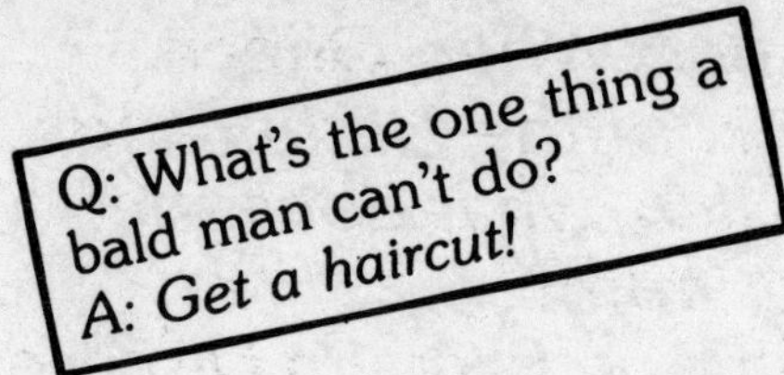

The Long and the Short of It

Two Boy Scouts were talking and one asked the other why summer days were longer than winter ones.

Quick as a flash the first boy replied, 'Easy! The heat of summer expands them and the cold of winter shrinks them.'

Teacher: What do you get if you eat expanded polystyrene foam?
Pupil: A little soft in the head.

I SAY, I SAY, I SAY . . .

I went to the optician's last week because of spots in front of my eyes. The bloke checked me over, told me I was short of sight and sold me a pair of specs. Now the spots are *much* clearer!

Cheap at the Price

Norton wanted to surprise his mum once, so he bought her a nice new TV. It was expensive - £300 - and he knew she wouldn't like it if he told her it cost so much, so he fibbed and said £50.

Two weeks later she called up and asked if he could get her some more.

Norton said, 'Some more what?'

She said, 'Some more of those fantastically cheap TVs. I sold mine for £100 and I know lots of other people who'll buy one too!'

I SAY, I SAY, I SAY . . .

That Derek's got a mind so shallow you could walk across it and still not get your feet wet.

Farmer Brown: Why is it always hard to take fresh cheese to market?
Farmer Green: Because it so often loses its whey!

I say, I say, I say. My dog hasn't got a nose!
So how does he smell?
He's got a machine for doing that!

I Know an Old Theory

I asked my friend Alex to explain Einstein's Theory of Relativity to me. He said that it was just like the way eight hours of solid homework always seemed much longer than eight hours of zonked-out sleep.

If that's a theory, I'll eat my hat!

3. Nuclear Power Jokes

Peckish

My friend Lily was feeling a mite peckish the other day, so she went to Costas' café and ordered a ham, tomato, cream cheese and mustard sandwich. As soon as it arrived she sank her teeth in it and immediately called the waitress back.

'What *are* you playing at?' she demanded.

'It's what you ordered, innit?' the waitress replied sweetly.

'Nothing wrong with the ham,' Lily said, picking some out of her ear. 'And I love the tomato and squishy cream cheese. The mustard is, of course, your usual eye-watering treat. But the bread is, without doubt, yesterday's.'

'You poor dear,' the waitress said, 'wasn't yesterday a good day for you?'

A Night Not Fit for Man Nor Beast

A kindly old vicar was taken very poorly and, as the weather outside was especially horrible just then, he asked his wife to get the vet.

'The vet? You must be delirious. You mean the doctor, don't you?' she replied.

'Oh no, I couldn't bring the doctor out on a night like this . . .' replied the vicar.

I SAY, I SAY, I SAY . . .

What's all this I hear about working shorter hours? If sixty minutes was good enough when I began, it's certainly good enough today!

Professor: If you spent three years at college taking medicine, what would you be?
Student: Better!

Cats and Dogs

Two girls were walking to school one day when it started to drizzle. Soon it was tipping down - it made a monsoon look like a lawn-sprinkler!

One girl was carrying an umbrella but she refused to open it.

'Why not?' asked her friend.

'I'm not going to bother,' the other girl replied, 'it's full of holes.'

'Well, *why* did you bring it?' asked her drenched friend.

'Because I didn't think it was going to rain!'

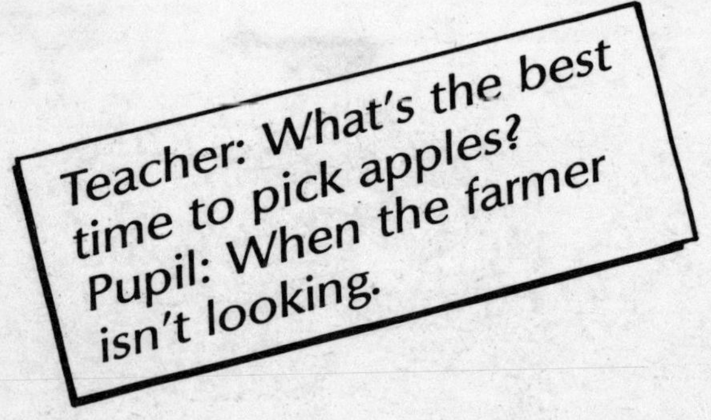

What did the squirrel say to the oak tree?
'Must we really have so many of these hilarious cakes, Quentin?'

Teacher: What do you think Prince Charles will do when he gets to the throne?
Pupil: Sit on it!

Nose to the Ground

A man went to the doctor to have some plastic surgery on his nose. As it turned out, the doctor could only take the graft from his bottom. Everything went fine, except that after the operation, whenever the man felt tired, he always tried to sit down on his face!

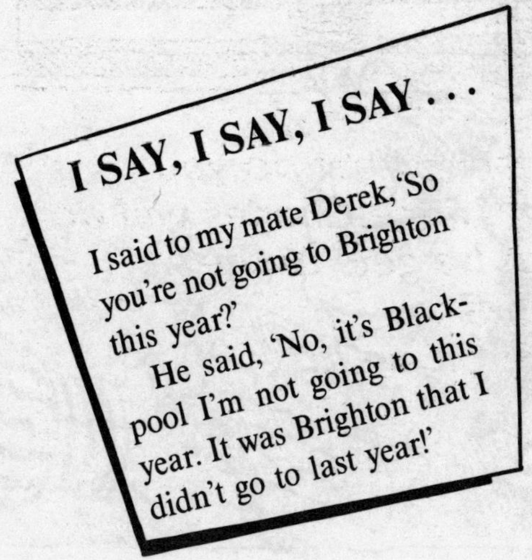

Just in the Nick of Time

This fellow's cheap watch stopped working one day, so he took it to the watchmaker.

'I've been a bit silly, I dropped my watch,' he said.

The watchmaker took a look at it. 'You probably couldn't help dropping it,' he replied. 'The silly bit was picking it up again.'

I SAY, I SAY, I SAY . . .

Let me ask you this. If you were in Paris and took it into your head to jump in the river, would you be mad or just in Seine?

Q: What's the best way to guarantee putting on weight?
A: *Swallow a plum whole — you'll gain a stone!*

What's in a Name?

A policeman came up to a man on a street corner and shoved a photo of a hunchback under his hooter. Well, after he'd taken a gander, the man said:

'Who's that?'

'Quasimodo,' said the cop.

'Quasimodo? Quasimodo?' said the man. 'That name rings a bell!'

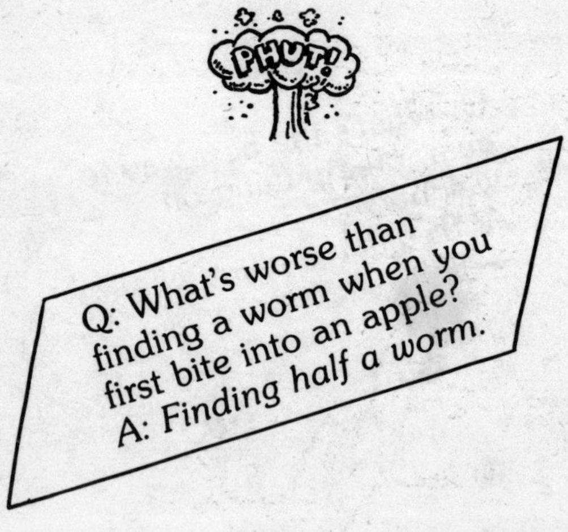

Q: What's worse than finding a worm when you first bite into an apple?
A: Finding *half* a worm.

What did the policeman with three heads say?
'It pays
to go for
big laughs.'

Fish Face

A furious fishmonger walked up to a man in the street and slapped him in the face with a wet haddock.

'That'll show you, Nigel, you total prat!'

His victim just burst out laughing, at which the man holding the fishy weapon threatened to hit him again.

'But can't you see how silly this is?' giggled the scale-covered fellow. 'I'm not Nigel!'

Silly Notice

A man went into an office building the other day, and in the foyer saw a big notice that said:

'IN CASE OF FIRE, DO NOT USE THE LIFTS!'

Silly instruction, he thought. Why not tell people to use the fire extinguisher instead?

Q: What does a cow with hiccups give you?
A: *Milkshakes.*

My friend Derek's favourite diet is the Arizona Sea Food Diet. Motto: Every time you see food, eat it.

4. Latest Test Match Jokes

A Cliffhanger Ending

A young German lad and his mother were walking along the top of a cliff when, all of a sudden, the mother slipped and fell over the edge.

The boy's friend came running over with a look of panic on his face. 'What happened?' he yelled.

'Look, Hans! No Ma!' came the reply.

Now Pull the Other Leg

A man called up his boss one morning and told him he couldn't come to work because of a broken leg. The boss ordered him in anyway, telling him it was a pretty lame excuse.

Teacher: I hope I didn't see you cheating in that exam, Jimmy.
Little Jimmy: So do I!

I SAY, I SAY, I SAY . . .

As my dear green mother used to say before she gave up the pipe: 'Where there's smoke, there's toast!'

Did you hear the one about the bloke whom everybody called Archie when he was little?
Now that he's grown up and lost all his hair, everyone calls him Archibald.

I SAY, I SAY, I SAY . . .

I trod on a bunch of grapes today. It didn't seem to mind at all — just gave out a little whine.

Funny old game, isn't it? Underwater hang-gliding.

Did you hear the one about the boxer who was so scared of going into the ring that he had a special pair of pants made?

They came up to his ears because he'd heard there was no punching below the belt.

Branching Out

This tall, dark and handsome Canadian fellow went for a job interview to be a lumberjack. The interviewer said he could have the job if he cut down a 20-foot tree in ten minutes.

No trouble — the Canadian did it in eight minutes. So he was told to fell a 40-foot one in under half an hour. He did it in fifteen minutes and didn't even break out into a sweat.

'Where'd you learn to cut down trees like that?' asked the interviewer.

'In the Kalahari Desert.'

'But there aren't any trees in the Kalahari!' exclaimed the interviewer.

'Shows you how well I learned!' said the lumberjack.

Shaggy Dog Collar Story

An awfully distressed lady rushed into a café shouting: 'Does anyone here own a large black dog with a white collar?'

There was no reply.

'Oh no!' wailed the poor lady. 'Then I must've run over the vicar!'

I SAY, I SAY, I SAY . . .

I went to the doctor complaining of an awful pain in my foot. He was busy and told me to hop it.

I can do four things all at once: sing, juggle tarpaulins, whittle like a silly boy, and lemons, cakes and cushions.

A Little Golf

Two women walked into a department store, and one of them stopped to pick up a golf ball.

'Don't bother with one. Take a pack of ten, it's cheaper!' said the assistant. 'And while you're at it, why don't you get a new set of clubs?'

'That's a good idea!' said the woman.

'And to make your life easy — how about a golf cart?'

'Just the thing!' agreed the woman.

'With all this new equipment, you wouldn't want to look like a tramp on the course — we have a terrific offer on sweaters, skirts and shoes.'

'I'll take a full set!' said the woman, busily writing out a cheque.

After she'd gone, the floor manager told the assistant that that was the finest piece of salesmanship he'd ever seen.

'She came in for one golf ball and walked out with half the shop!' said the manager.

'A golf ball?' said the assistant. 'She came in looking for our travel agency because she wanted a weekend's holiday. So I said, "A weekend break? Why not play a little golf while you're away?"'

Being Honest

Two newspaper boys were arguing with each other about who was the most honest.

'So you see, there are lots of ways to make money, but there's only *one* honest one!' said the first boy.

'And what might that be?' asked the second.

'Hah!' yelled the first boy. 'I knew it! You don't know!'

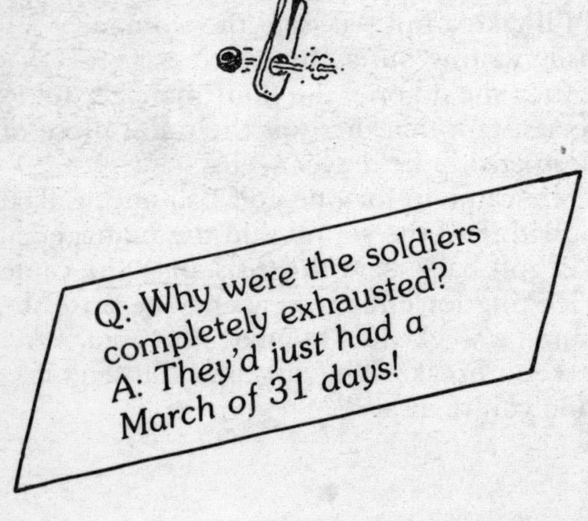

I SAY, I SAY, I SAY . . .

When I was young I tried to run away with the circus. It was too heavy, so I gave up and went home.

Derek's sister went to dance school where they told her that only two things could get in the way of her being a world-famous dancer.

Her feet.

Q: What kind of spook can only be found on the tip of your finger?
A: A bogey.

Knock, knock!
Eh who?
Eh?
Eh? I can't hear you . . . I'm a long way away!

Did you hear the one about the ghost who was seen leaving a restaurant in a terrible huff?

The waiters wouldn't serve spirits!

5. Baked Bean Jokes

See Him Fired!

A young salesman walked into the boss's office one morning without knocking.

The boss yelled at him, 'Much too busy now! I can't see you!'

To which the young fellow snapped back, 'Well, today's your lucky day — I'm an optician!'

I SAY, I SAY, I SAY . . .

I have a friend with a huge market garden. As winter approaches, he eats what he can and cans what he can't.

Did you hear the one about the man who took his clock to the psychiatrist because it suddenly went cuckoo?

Tooth Furry

A park-keeper was walking through the park one day when he saw a little girl with a dog.

'Does your dog bite?' he asked her.

'No,' said the girl.

Just then, the mangy mutt sank its jaws into his leg.

'You told me your dog doesn't bite!' yelped the parkie.

'It doesn't,' replied the girl. 'But this isn't my dog!'

Who Me? Snore??

A man went to the doctor complaining that he snored so loudly he woke himself up.

The doctor told him he should sleep in the room next door, where the noise wouldn't disturb him so much.

I SAY, I SAY, I SAY . . .

What I want to know is this — does a dying man who wants to be cremated have one foot in the grate?

'Doc,' said the patient. 'Every time I drink a cup of tea I get a sharp pain in my eye.'

'Have you tried taking the spoon out of the cup?' sighed the doctor.

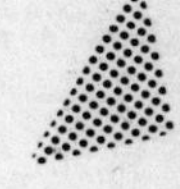

At the Track

There was a report in the newspaper of a race between a teacher, a tap and a bottle of tomato sauce.

By the last lap the teacher was a head, the tap was running slowly, and the sauce was trying to ketchup.

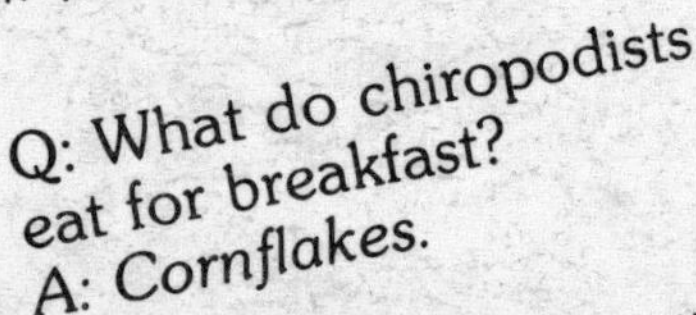

Q: What do chiropodists eat for breakfast?
A: Cornflakes.

Man cannot live by bread alone. He has to move in with loads of other people.

I SAY, I SAY, I SAY . . .

There's only one thing worse than being with a fool, and that's fooling with a bee.

Q: What would a ghost be most likely to say if it appeared in your room?
A: *'Just passing through.'*

Flash With a Pan

Mr Shepherd is a real cordon bleu wizard in the kitchen. You name it, he can cook it beautifully.

One day a friend went to stay with him and, while there, the budgie died. Hey presto! Budgie curry for lunch. The next day all the gerbils kicked the bucket; for supper they sat down to magnificent southern-fried gerbil.

On the third day, Mr Shepherd's mum passed away. At that point, his friend packed his bags and left, muttering something about Shepherd's pie not being to his taste at all.

Club Mosquito

A French millionaire once went on a jungle holiday, Club Mosquito or something, and one day he had a terrific stand-up argument with a tiger.

That night the other holiday-makers were woken up by awful screams coming from his hut. When they rushed in, all that was left of him was a mangled mess. It seems that something he'd disagreed with, ate him!

I SAY, I SAY, I SAY . . .

I spent a week in the country recently. It was so cold that the foxes were killing chickens, plucking them and using the feathers to make duvets.

Q: How does Frankenstein's monster usually like to sit?
A: *Bolt upright!*

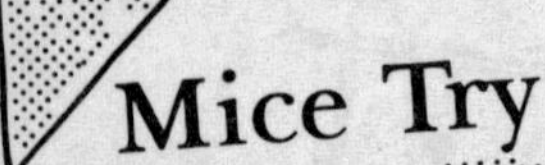

Mice Try

The salesman in a pet shop sold my Uncle Hubert a cat the other day. He told him it'd be good for the mice. After a week of it having caught not a single, solitary little squeaker, Hubert went back and complained.

'Well,' said the salesman, 'I told you it'd be good for the mice!'

I SAY, I SAY, I SAY . . .

My friend Norman grew up thinking that happiness was a personal jet, tons of money and a hamburger restaurant of his own. He was right!

Knock, knock!
Who's there?
Leonard Drummond.
Hello, Leonard, you old pit pony.

Zoo Story
Two kangaroos were standing around in the zoo one day, when one said to the other:
'I just *hate* it when it rains and the kids have to play indoors!'

Henry sat down in a posh restaurant and said to the waiter:

'I've only got five pounds with me. What do you recommend?'

'Another restaurant,' said the waiter.

6. Hilarious DJ Jokes

If you go down to the woods today you're sure for a big surprise. What with all those fish and that!

7. Elephant Jokes

Knock, knock!
Who's there?
Dishwasher.
Dishwasher who?
Dishwashern't de way I shpoke before I had falsh teesh.

Teacher: 'If you buried someone in the wrong cemetery, what would you have made?
Pupil: 'A grave mistake.'

Frankenstein's Buddy

Dr Frankenstein is one of those people who's never lonely, because he has such a terrific talent for making friends.

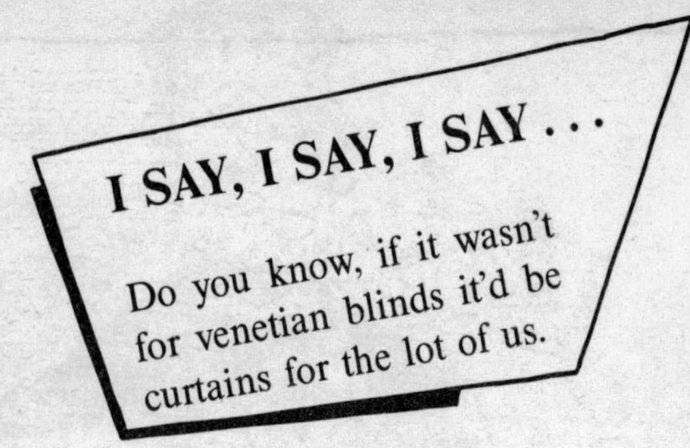

Here, Kitty!

Did you hear about the cowboy who was captured by the dreaded Hole-in-the-Wall Gang? They had him staked out in the sun and were getting ready to watch him die a slow and horrible death, when he asked for one last request. Could he have a word with his horse?

The bandits were feeling generous and so they allowed him a quick word with his nag. As soon as the conversation was over, the horse turned and galloped away.

The bandits were slightly puzzled by this, but were even more so when the horse returned an hour later clutching a small, fluffy kitten in its mouth.

The cowboy seemed as surprised as his captors and asked for one more word with his horse. As the horse bent down to listen to what his master had to say, the bandits heard him hiss loudly:

'I said *posse*, you numbskull, not *pussy*!'

Waiter Bit

A man was brought to hospital after being bitten by a mad dog that had somehow made it into the restaurant where he was having lunch.

When the doctor told him he was suffering from rabies he went bright purple and tried to rush out of the ward.

'Where do you think you're going?' grunted the doctor, pushing him back into bed.

'I want to get back to that restaurant,' the man said, 'to bite the rotten swine who let the dog in!'

I SAY, I SAY, I SAY . . .

My place got broken into the other night, and when the policeman asked how the burglar entered, I told him — intruder window!

One day in the playground a boy boasted to another:

'My dad's stronger than your dad,' he said, 'he's a weightlifter.'

'That's nothing,' said the friend, 'my dad's twice as strong — he's a shoplifter.'

Did you hear the one about the customer in a restaurant who told the head waiter that he had a complaint?

The waiter told him to go down the road to the hospital.

Lucky Break

A gamekeeper at a safari park saw a woman being chased by a lion one day. As she galloped past him, he shouted:

'Don't worry, lady! He looks like a man-eater to me!'

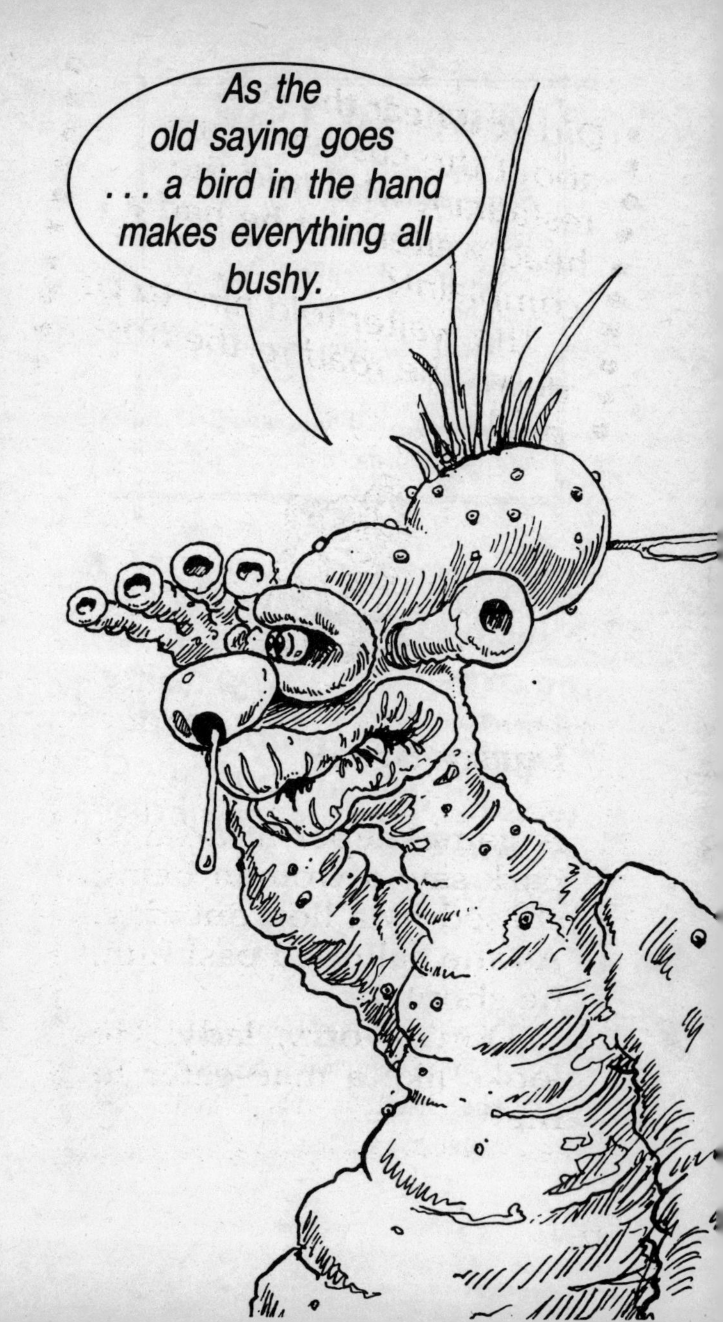
As the
old saying goes
. . . a bird in the hand
makes everything all
bushy.

I SAY, I SAY, I SAY . . .

Someone once asked me if I was any good at quantum mechanics. I replied, 'Yes and no.'

'What do you mean?' they said.

'I mean yes, I'm no good at quantum mechanics.'

'I can't find any oxtail in my oxtail soup!' complained Derek to the waiter.

'Big deal!' grumbled the waiter. 'Would you expect to find a horse in the horse-radish sauce?'

I was told that Henry VIII had so many wives because he liked to chop and change.

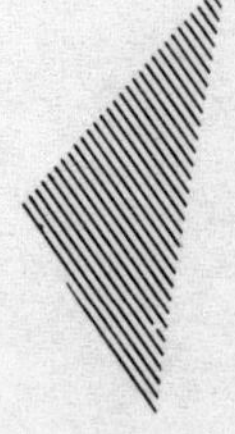

Q: What do you call fifty builders falling off a roof?
A: A navvylanche!

Better or Worse

Did you hear the one about a man in hospital who woke up feeling so much better after an operation that he asked if he could dance. Soon afterwards he did a little turn for the nurse.

Q: What do you get if you cross a birthday cake with a plate of beans?
A: Candles that blow themselves out!

Just at that moment, the vicar's vest exploded!

'You remind me of my favourite boxer,' said Anna to Terry who was getting on her nerves.

'Oh,' said Terry, puffing up his chest. 'Do you mean Frank Bruno?'

'Nope,' replied Anna. 'Fido.'

8. Dead Gerbil Jokes

Parcel Post

A young woman went to the post office to get some stamps for a parcel.

'Shall I stick them on myself?' she asked the man behind the counter.

'Well, I *usually* recommend sticking them on the parcel, madam,' he replied.

Did you hear the one about the home economics teacher who asked her class to name five things containing starch?

Up shot the hand of one of her pupils. 'Miss, miss! How about three shirts and two collars!'

Trench Warfare

There once was a building site foreman who was so desperate for help that he hired three lunatics to work for him. Their first job was to dig a trench.

When the foreman went to check on how they were doing, he found one man working and the other two standing on either side of him with their picks up in the air.

'What's going on here?' he yelled.

'We're the floodlights,' replied one of the lunatics.

'Don't be so *stupid*!' the foreman bellowed, and promptly sacked the two men. As they got out of the trench and walked away, the third man stopped working and climbed out too.

'Where do you think you're going?' asked the foreman.

'Well,' said the madman, 'I can't be expected to work in the dark, now can I?'

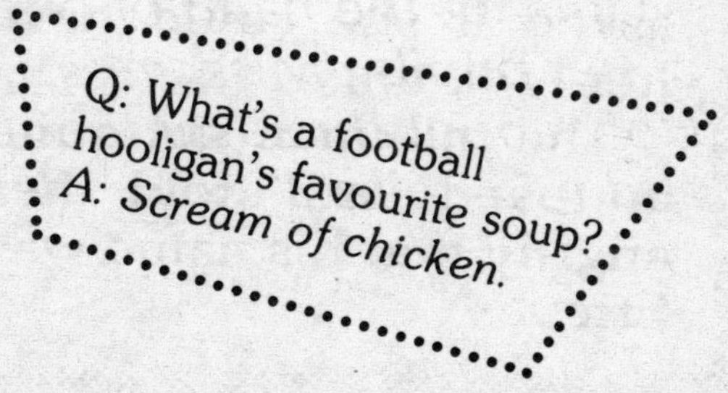

Did you hear the one about the naughty boy whose mum told him to stop kicking the neighbour's new furniture? She made him stop because he'd scuff his best shoes.

Eric the Red-Faced

A woman stopped the milkman one morning and asked if she could have her milk bill.

The milkman got quite annoyed and told her angrily that his name was Eric.

As the
old saying goes
. . . a bird in the hand
makes for a messy
wrist!

No Dust Up

A young teacher gave up his job to become a trainee door-to-door hoover salesman. He went to his first house, knocked on the door and waited until it was opened. Then he threw a bag of dirt into the hall.

'Have *I* got an incredible machine for you, sir!' he beamed at the dumbfounded homeowner, and he held up his latest model hoover.

'It had better be,' the man growled. 'My electricity's just been cut off!'

Meals on Legs

Did you hear the one about the cowboy who rode up to the chuck wagon and told everybody he was so hungry he could eat a horse?

His steed promptly swished its tail and said, 'Meow!'

'We're about to cross the Forth Bridge,' said Johnny's dad, pointing out the car window.

'That's strange,' said Johnny. 'I don't remember crossing the other three!'

I've been all over the world, and I've seen everything there is to see, and there's only one thing left that I've got to do.
Yup!